Maximum Engagement

Moving Members, Customers, and Donors to Ever-Increasing Levels of Participation

C. DAVID GAMMEL, CAE

The Center for Association Leadership

WASHINGTON, DC

Information in this book is accurate as of the time of publication and consistent with standards of good practice in the general management community. As research and practice advance, however, standards may change. For this reason, it is recommended that readers evaluate the applicability of any recommendation in light of particular situations and changing standards.

ASAE: The Center for Association Leadership
1575 I Street, NW
Washington, DC 20005-1103
Phone: 202-371-0940 (when calling from within the Washington, D.C. metropolitan area)
Phone: 888-950-2723 (when calling from outside the Washington, D.C. metropolitan area)
Fax: 202-220-6439
Email: books@asaecenter.org

ASAE: The Center for Association Leadership connects great ideas to great people to inspire leadership and achievement within the association community.

Keith C. Skillman, CAE, Vice President, Publications, ASAE: The Center for Association Leadership
Baron Williams, CAE, Director, Book Publishing, ASAE: The Center for Association Leadership

A complete catalog of ASAE titles is available online at www.asaecenter.org/bookstore.

Cover design by Beth Lower
Interior design by Cimarron Design, cimarrondesign.com

International Standard Book Number, 10 digit: 0-88034-334-6
International Standard Book Number, 13 digit: 978-0-88034-334-3

Printed in the United States of America.
10 9 8 7 6 5 4 3 2 1

For Jennifer,
the best engagement decision
I ever made!

CONTENTS

INTRODUCTION

THIS BOOK STARTED AS a comment on a blog post, which was tweeted a few times. I then wrote a couple of posts expanding the comment on my own blog. This led to the opportunity to write a feature article on the topic in the May 2010 issue of ASAE's *Associations Now*. And now it has become this very book in your hands (or on your computer screen).

We need to approach engagement with our members, customers, and donors in much the same way. That is, we need to invite initial involvement with our organization and then deliberately nurture that interaction into greater participation through purchase and use of our products and services, involvement in leadership, donations, and support of our mission. What can we do to accelerate that process?

The more time and money that people invest with our organizations, the best evidence of engagement, the more we can contribute to our missions and build the financial strength required for sustained success. The reason this works so well as a measure is that the money and time continue to flow to us only if value is flowing back to the individuals giving those precious resources to us. If time and money are coming in on a growing basis, you are almost certainly delivering more value to your most important members, customers, donors, and constituents.

My intent is that this book will help you to frame the challenge and opportunity of engagement for your organization, enabling you to take specific actions that will support both your mission and bottom line through enhanced engagement with your supporters and market.

As a rather famous starship captain often started his next adventure, "Engage!"

CHAPTER 1

Engagement:
It's What We Do

MANY ORGANIZATIONS OPERATE AS if they are a conglomerate of small businesses, all targeted at a highly focused market, with a consensus-based governance model slapped on top. The great management challenge in this scenario is determining the proper mix of these businesses and effectively moving people among them.

Organizations that take this to the level of an art form focus on providing highly enticing initial offers of value to their best prospects and then accelerate them through a progression of their offerings. Let's explore this using the example of bra colors being posted in Facebook updates.

(Stick with me; I promise to tie this in!)

In January of 2010, updates like these started showing up in Facebook profiles: blue, pink, beige, blue with little white flowers, red. Someone, and no one knows who, had the idea that women should post their bra color in their status update without any explanation. The purpose of doing so was to raise awareness of, and support for curing, breast cancer. Before you knew it, the meme took off like a Breck shampoo commercial on fast forward, with hundreds of thousands of women posting their bra color to their Facebook status.

Once the meme hit the news, fundraising professionals questioned the efficacy of the "campaign." There was no call to action, they said. There was no next step that people were encouraged to take once awareness on this issue was heightened. And they were quite right: There was no call to action. The meme was about awareness for awareness's sake, as could be conceived only by someone outside of an organization. There was even pushback by friends of those who posted their bra color, putting out their own updates about how this was a rather meaningless task.

In the midst of all this, something interesting happened to the Susan G. Komen Foundation fan page on Facebook: They went from a few hundred fans to more than 100,000 fans. In one day. That is not a typo. It turns out that women posting their bra color to Facebook were primed and ready to do something more meaningful, and Komen was in that space with a mission and brand perfectly aligned with the self-forming parade that had just occurred. Bingo! A huge influx of fans came, looking for that next slightly more meaningful step they could take to support breast cancer awareness.

Komen could not have instigated this grassroots response, even with a massive campaign. It would have been laughed out of the meeting room most likely and, even if it did move forward, would have fallen flat with this very same audience. Authenticity gets bandied about a lot when social media are discussed, but the bra color meme is a great example of it: something that is created independently and then spreads by word of mouth. What Komen did do that contributed to this success was to have a presence on

Facebook with many options built in for advancing engagement with people who encountered them there. They had control over this bit of Facebook and built it in an intelligent way, which allowed them to create tremendous value from the meme when it took off. Without that work, they would have realized very little from this.

What we are really talking about is finding people who are best aligned with your mission and purpose (and making it easy for them to find you) and engaging with them in common pursuits. Those with close alignment to our goals will happily increase their level of engagement with us, as more than 100,000 people did with the Susan G. Komen Foundation on Facebook.

Let's talk a bit about what engagement is, how you can recognize it when you see it, and why it is important.

What Is Engagement?

The term *engagement* is often bandied about in the marketing and communications world. More engagement is considered better, yet we rarely state what that actually means or why it truly matters.

I define engagement as the following: *Engagement is the result of a person investing time and/or money with the organization in exchange for value.* The more of these precious resources invested in the organization, the more engaged he or she is with the organization. Someone who speaks at a lot of conferences and writes many articles for a publication is highly engaged. Another person who invests hundreds of thousands of dollars in donations or sponsorship money is also highly engaged, even if she does absolutely nothing else.

Engagement is about value—the value for the person doing the engaging as well as the value of that engagement for the association.

Why Does Engagement Matter?

Engagement is evidence of success and provides fuel for your mission and future growth. Members, customers, and others investing in the organization demonstrate perceived high value. Properly structured, such investment will give the organization the financial and human capital it needs to achieve goals and maximize contributions to its mission.

Consistently healthy organizations create more engagement opportunities in areas with strategic value for the organization. Having a surfeit of articles to publish is nice but doesn't really matter if your organization has been losing money for the last three years. Susan G. Komen has created a variety of engagement opportunities that they were able to offer to their newly acquired Facebook audience. Without those options, that momentary attention they received would have been just that: a blip in time with no long-term impact for them.

Successful Organizations Create Engagement Where It Matters

If you accept that engagement occurs when someone invests time or money with the organization in exchange for value, you can then consider opportunities to do so on a continuum of value, from low to high. Viewing a web page to becoming a member to sponsoring the organization becomes a series of stations along an engagement progression path, rather than isolated destinations.

Examples of early stops along the engagement path might include

- viewing content on your website, blog, Twitter feed, Facebook fan page, and so forth;

- paying attention to a public service announcement or press
  coverage; and
- sharing content from your website or other publication.

Examples of mid-level engagement, of much higher individual value, could include

- buying a product;
- attending a conference or event;
- applying for a job via your career center; and
- writing or speaking.

The highest levels of engagement could include any of the following:

- volunteering for a committee or task force
- serving in a leadership role
- receiving recognition such as fellowship or other achievement status
- spending significant money on sponsorship, advertising, exhibit space, and so forth

The important concept here from a strategy perspective is to plot out what lower-value engagement activities and options will feed into higher levels and how you can progress people through them. Imagine professional baseball without the minor leagues. Moving all players from high school or college straight to major league teams (aside from the rare exceptional talents) would be very hard to do well. The minors provide an important talent channel for the majors. While I'm not suggesting you develop your own minor league, you do need to consider how people will progress as their relationship with you matures.

Organizations with an efficient flow from low- to high-value engagement will tend to be healthier from both revenue and mission-fulfillment perspectives. This engagement flow can be visualized as a curve, so that as the number of people engaged in an activity decreases, the value of the engagement for all parties increases. I call this the *engagement acceleration curve*, which the next chapter describes in detail.

Organizational management is largely about creating engagement opportunities and then marketing them to those most likely to value them. It is literally what we do most of the time as executives and management in all types of organizations.

What We've Got Here Is Failure to Engage

The sadistic prison warden in the movie *Cool Hand Luke* famously said, "What we've got here is failure to communicate," before inflicting more punishment on Paul Newman's character. The ability to generate engagement is critical to resiliency in the world of today. Failing to grow engagement with your members, donors, and constituents ultimately leads to stagnation and failure as an organization. Let's explore why this is the case more so today than it ever has been in the past.

It's become an old bromide that the pace of change is constantly increasing. If you look at the events of the past few years, it is patently true. With a world that changes so quickly, no one organization can rely on what worked yesterday continuing to work tomorrow. Here are just a few of the events that represent rapid change:

- Bernie Madoff's pyramid scheme collapses, taking numerous foundations and nonprofits down with it.

- The Dow Jones Industrial Average hit a low point of 6,547.05 on March 9, 2009.
- The Dow closed over 11,000 in April of 2010.
- Amazon.com launched the Kindle, selling eBooks for its device as well as Kindle software on a variety of platforms, roiling the print business.
- Three million iPads were sold by Apple in the first few months after its release, also roiling the print business (I think my grandmother could roil the print business at this point).
- The first African-American was elected president of the United States.
- Projections estimate there will be 5 billion mobile phone accounts in the world, for a population just shy of 7 billion people.
- Afghanistan became the longest war in U.S. history.

I think the utter tragedy of the Bernie Madoff scheme was that so many foundations and charities were either directly invested with him or received the lion's share of their funding from people who had their money with this fraud. This lack of diversification in both investments and income sources doomed these organizations to massive cutbacks at best or oblivion at worst. It provides a perfect lesson in why diversification of engagement is critical: It lets you recover when one of your sources dries up or loses interest in you. If you have only one source of engagement, even if it does a lot for you, your organization is in a precarious position.

What It Takes for People to Renew Membership

What is the single greatest reason why people fail to renew membership? Failure to perceive enough value to justify the dues investment, by a country mile.[1] Diversification of value offered to your customers, members, and donors provide many reasons to remain engaged, rather than a single good one not to.

The world does not hold still. Nor can you afford to either. Those who can consistently create and accelerate engagement among their constituents will be able to survive the vicissitudes of finance, war, and natural disasters. Equally important, they are able to leverage the numerous opportunities that present themselves to us every day.

Exercise: High Value Engagement

Here is an exercise to begin thinking about the engagement opportunities your organization has to offer.

1. List the three highest-value forms of engagement that you offer. They may be in the form of time, money, or both.
2. List the three lowest-value forms of engagement that you offer.
3. Consider how well you do in moving people from those low-value opportunities to the highest value.

Getting people from the lowest to the highest may seem like an insurmountable jump. However, as we'll discuss in the rest of the book, creating an engagement process is the key to doing so consistently and effectively.

---

[1] *The Decision to Join*, Dalton and Dignam, ASAE, 2007, p. 24.

CHAPTER 2

The Engagement Acceleration Curve: Engaging with Intent

ONE OF THE CHALLENGES about the concept of engagement is that it has been so squishy for so long. What is it? Why does it matter? How does it fit into the big picture of what we want to achieve as an organization? I developed a visual tool that will help you understand that engagement is really a process rather than a single event. I call this tool the *engagement acceleration curve.*

The engagement acceleration curve is a classic double axis chart, illustrating the progression from low- to high-value engagement with the organization by its constituents. The vertical axis shows the number of people involved in a particular engagement activity, the number of people increasing as you move upward from the origin. The horizontal axis shows increasing levels of engagement (measured by time or money exchanged with the organization) as you move away from the origin to the right.

The curve that is mapped out in Figure 2.1 shows that as the number of people increases, the value of engagement tends to increase. Throughout my career, I've yet to run across an organization that did not generally follow this same power law curve: As the number of people engaging decreases, the value of the engagement for them and the organization increases.

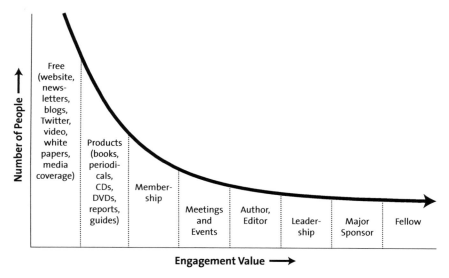

Figure 2.1: Engagement Acceleration Curve

The secret of the most successful executives is that they create their organization's curve by design rather than by default. The Society for Human Resource Management (SHRM) experienced explosive growth in the 1990s when the President & CEO at the time, Mike Losey, led an effort to bring a vastly larger percentage of the human resource community into the fold. They did this through creating a diverse array of offerings and marketing them effectively, engaging more people overall, and maximizing the value delivered to the market in total.

Engagement curves can be designed to accelerate people from low- to high-value engagement activities with your organization, like a downhill skier gaining momentum as she starts down the slope. The curve in Figure 2.1 provides an example for a hypothetical association showing how you can progress smoothly from free content, available to the most people, through various stages of engagement until you reach the highest levels, which in this case includes lifetime recognition by becoming a Fellow of the organization; this represents the pinnacle of recognition for many membership organizations. (See Appendix A: The Big List of Engagement Ideas and Their Values for more information about filling out and accelerating engagement with your constituents.)

Origins of the Curve

This type of curve is certainly not new and is commonly referred to as a power law in mathematics, where frequency varies according to some other attribute. I gleaned the idea of using it to represent accelerating business value and relationships from Alan Weiss's consulting community. In 2006, Christopher Anderson, editor of

Wired magazine, used power law curves in his book *The Long Tail*, although this conception is a bit different in that you use the "hits" of free or inexpensive content and services to move to the "niche" offerings for which you actually charge. We'll come back to Anderson again in a bit.

The power of visualizing engagement like this is that you can quickly map out the offerings of your organization and determine how well you are progressing people from low to high engagement. In practice, marketers can use this to guide their communications so that people can be targeted for the next offer in your curve. Trading a bit of value in exchange for an email address and permission to communicate is a fantastic step that then opens up many long-term possibilities for building high-value engagement.

One foundation executive pointed out to me that once you have a healthy curve in place, if you add a bunch of the right people to the beginning of it, the entire thing moves up. This creates tremendous value throughout the system for those engaging with you and therefore for your mission and bottom line. This is just what the Susan G. Komen Foundation did with their runaway success of a Facebook fan page. They were able to leverage this unanticipated gift of manna from heaven by using the fan page to launch people into greater engagement with the foundation.

Exercise: Engagement Inventory

Gather a list of all engagement points with your organization, where someone gives time and/or money to you in exchange for some form of value. The items in your list should be at a high level and may represent aggregated activities, such as grouping a class of products or similar volunteer activities together.

Note the following for each engagement item:

- total estimated revenue, if any, generated by the item in a single year
- amount of time it takes for someone to engage in the activity or item
- total number of people you estimate engage with each item or activity in a single year

You can define a time period that you will analyze, which can be for a month, year, or multiple years. Here are a few examples for a 12-month period to help you get started:

- **Website Visitors.** Total online revenue, average time on site, total unique visitors in last 12 months
- **Membership.** Total membership dues, estimate of average time spent using membership services, total number of members
- **Webinar.** Registration revenue, length of webinar, total registrants
- **Board of Directors Member.** Money donated to organization (if your board members typically do this; otherwise revenue may be zero), time spent per board member conducting board duties, total number of board members

Rough estimates of the above are fine for high-level planning purposes. All of these data can easily be compiled in a spreadsheet, with a column for each item name, revenue, time, and number of people. This will allow the list to be easily sorted while you work on developing your own engagement curve. Precision in the data you collect is not as important as making sure that all the significant classes of activities, products, services, programs, and other engagement opportunities are covered. (See Appendix A: The Big List of Engagement Ideas and Their Values for more information.)

Some items may be redundant as well, such as revenue gathered online versus revenue for specific programs paid for via the web. You should note this where appropriate, but don't worry too much about it. The goal in this exercise is to understand the impact of various experiences open to your constituents rather than a formal accounting of cash flow.

CHAPTER 3

Feeding the Curve: Free Must Lead to Fee

MY GRANDFATHER, JD GAMMEL, Sr., marketed successfully with free in the rural America of the 1940s. As the tale goes, JD Senior had started a small appliance store in the early 1940s and was trying to sell his stock of new electric ice boxes. He lived in western Kentucky which was in the midst of significant change as the Rural Electrification Administration set up electric cooperatives that ran wires out like spokes from a hub during the period when the Tennessee Valley Authority built hydro-electric dams across the middle of the United States.

Granddad would load a few electric ice boxes into the back of his pickup truck and follow the newly strung lines out into the countryside. He would stop at a modest farmhouse and ask if the man of the house was about. (Early '40s, remember!) If so, they would shoot the breeze for quite some time until finally the farmer would ask what he had in the pickup truck. The farmer, who was using electricity to light a bulb or two in his home, if that, was always skeptical. "We don't need an electric ice box! Our root cellar has worked for my family for as long as I can remember."

Granddad would admit as to how that was true but offered to leave one of his boxes on the farmer's front porch for a week at no cost and with no obligation. He would come back and take it away if they didn't want it. Novelty usually won out and he would leave with one less ice box in his pickup truck.

As you might foresee, while the farmer thought the root cellar was fine, his wife had a very different idea once they had the electric box in place. No mess, fresh cold milk, ice on demand, less spoiled food, and so on.

Granddad would come by the next week and the farmer would arrange a plan to pay him for the new electric ice box. Every single time. As the old saying goes, if Mama ain't happy, ain't nobody happy!

Free offerings are not new. Whether it's a sample or a tryout, marketers have been using free to generate business for generations. What I love about my Granddad's story is that it is a direct antecedent to modern offers of free services and technology online. Those electrical lines, strung as part of the recovery spending enacted during the Great Depression, were the precursors to modern networked communication. Those lines splayed out into the countryside, connecting farms and homes to the electrical grid. Soon telephone lines followed, and decades later that same copper could be used to get computers onto the internet.

The challenge of traditional free offerings was the high marginal cost of each free item. A free trial of an electric ice box requires having one in stock to begin with, then finding someone to try it, and then leaving it there for a week. This doesn't scale very well: My grandfather could put only so many ice boxes in circulation at one time, even if he had a couple more people with trucks.

Social Media Provides New Opportunities

This is the truly radical change that the internet and world wide web have wrought on marketing: Free can now scale to a level that might as well be infinite for any organization, publisher, or even individual. Christopher Anderson, in the book *Free*, argues that entirely new business models are now possible, given that the cost of providing content and services online is so low. Think of your own website. Serving up an additional page or even providing full access to your members-only archives has no meaningful marginal cost. This is a huge shift in business, commerce, and society. And it makes for some powerful new ways to attract your prospects and engage with them.

This is not to say that the creation of content itself is free. As the amount and velocity of online content continues to grow, it's essential to publish very high quality material of unique value to your target audiences. This enables you to rise above the cacophony of the mediocre online. However, with that base investment, it will cost you essentially nothing to offer it to more people via online channels. That is where the power of free kicks in: It lets you leverage your content investment to a much greater degree than ever possible before.

If we go back to the Susan G. Komen Foundation, as of this writing they had over 228,000 fans on their Facebook fan page. This is about 227,700 more than they had just a few months ago. This is a massive injection of new people into the beginning of their engagement curve. The fan page has numerous additional offers for visitors to take advantage of, each of which progresses them along to a slightly higher bit of engagement. Options include signing up for a free email newsletter, buying a sponsored product, registering for a charity walk, and more.

You get the idea. Use free content and services as a highly attractive entrée to what your organization has to offer. This is one of the great opportunities that social media provides to associations.

Pair Free with Next Actions

The absolutely most critical aspect of free is to have a very clear strategy on what you want someone to do next after they access the free value. Without that, you are wasting the investment of providing the free value, and significant opportunities are lost with every person who becomes an ephemeral drive-by rather than an increasingly engaged contributor to the organization.

Since offering free content and services online is so cheap, even with initial production factored in, I've seen many organizations get too enamored with creating and distributing free content without a clear strategy for how it will pay off for them. You have 10,000 fans on Facebook! Great! But so what? Have those fans done anything else with you? Do you have specific offers for them like Susan G. Komen had lined up? If not, you are missing a key point: Free must lead to fee. Despite being very low cost, free offerings do require cognitive overhead.

Cognitive Overhead

Cognitive overhead is the effort required to both develop and manage free offerings as well as the volume of offerings you are making to your constituents. The more offerings, the more effort in managing them or in figuring out which to access as a customer or constituent. The way to avoid this is to concentrate your efforts with specific next steps that you want people to take when they interact or experience your free offerings online. If you can't identify what that next step is or the free offering fails to produce it, then you should drop it and try something else.

The Air Conditioning Contractors of America (ACCA) released a free iPhone app in July of 2010, called *ACCA Today*. The app provides recent headlines and news from the organization as well as videos that they publish. The app grabs headlines and content from a variety of sources from ACCA, primarily via RSS feeds, and gives a nice presentation of them for the iPhone all in one easily accessible app.

The primary objectives of the *ACCA Today* app include

- getting the app on the phones of as many relevant people as possible;
- providing quick and easy access to ACCA's most recent and valuable content;
- driving membership sign-ups from those who are good prospects based on valuing this content; and
- generating display advertising revenue.

The interesting thing about this app from ACCA is that it was developed quickly by leveraging the results of long-term work on ACCA's website. Kevin Holland, ACCA's division vice president for business operations and membership, had migrated the association's websites to the Wordpress platform, which natively supports RSS feeds by category of content. ACCA leveraged this ability to create an app that drew content from their magazine, as posted to Wordpress, via categorized RSS feeds. Thus, ACCA built and launched the app in just a few days using the AppMakr service (www.appmakr.com) by leveraging years of work on making their online content easy to syndicate.

The upshot is that their free content online, forming a key component of the left-hand side of their engagement acceleration curve, can easily be pulled into new platforms and offerings, such as this iPhone app. This will draw more traffic from their closest followers and provides both potential revenue as well as fueling acceleration toward higher engagement activities such as membership, conference attendance, or grassroots advocacy efforts.

Some organizations are successful with free offerings even when the marginal cost involved in delivering the free service is expensive. Organizations as disparate as the National Defense Industrial Association (NDIA) and the Ohio Society of CPAs (OSCPA) both use free membership as a method for accelerating engagement. OSCPA gives a free one-year membership to newly minted CPAs in the state and then communicates with them about the value of that membership to their career and profession throughout the trial year. J. Clarke Price, CAE, Executive Director of the association, reported that the free one-year membership program is "accelerating the speed with which we bring new CPAs into the membership and increasing the capture rate on renewals."[1] Thomas Nordby, Assistant Vice President of Operations at NDIA, told me that they use free individual membership offers to market corporate memberships as well as targeted educational offerings. The results of both of these campaigns far outweigh the cost of delivering physical products (such as a magazine) and other benefits to free members. These are great examples of how an engagement acceleration strategy can be put into productive action with the use of free.

The Website as Engagement Flywheel

A flywheel is used to store energy that can be tapped and applied as needed. It is used to accelerate other things. Jim Collins popularized the idea in management in his book, *Good to Great,* saying that great organizations have a flywheel that they add momentum to slowly over time and then use it to fuel their growth by applying that energy in focused ways.

One way to think of your website is as an *engagement flywheel.* Engagement occurs when someone trades time or money with your organization for value. While the website itself can provide limitless engagement opportunities, its more powerful function may be to accelerate website visitors so that they engage further with the organization in more valuable ways. (See Appendix A: The Big List of Engagement Ideas and Their Values for more information on generating ideas on how to fill out and accelerate engagement with your constituents.)

---

[1] "CEO to CEO," *Associations Now,* February 2010.

When your best prospective members, customers, or advocates come to your site for the first time, what is the very next thing they should do that would build engagement, putting them on the path to greater involvement and value with you? Focusing your site on those types of outcomes will turn it into an engagement flywheel, giving momentum to the people you most want to draw into your organization.

While the website can assist in almost any level of engagement, its true power is on the left side of the engagement curve. You can serve essentially an infinite audience online with free content, converting the best prospects among them to the next step in engagement with you. Having clarity on those precise steps is critical. The site can also fuel sales of products and services as your constituents move along the curve to higher levels.

In many cases, free content and services might actually lead to action by your visitors rather than a cash transaction. The key is to enable and encourage actions that are desired by your constituents and highly valued by your organization. President Barack Obama's campaign organization provides a great example with its iPhone app.

Case: Grassroots Advocacy App

Barack Obama's campaign organization, Organizing for America (OFA), has an iPhone app out that does a great job at a few things, which is just what you want in a mobile app. Mobile apps have to leverage the unique value and constraints of mobile, networked devices if they are to gain traction.

OFA's app focuses on giving activists who support its agenda the information and tools they need to be active in a common cause.

The app provides news, local event information, photos and videos, discussion points, and a tool with which to contact Congress.

Those are all the data and action points a grassroots advocate needs to actually take action. Regardless of your politics, this is a great model for anyone who does advocacy work to examine.

The Business Case for Social Media

Social media is part and parcel of the explosion of free content and services online. When placed in the context of engagement, social media can serve a profound role in attracting and sustaining engagement with your best prospects, members, donors, customers, and other you wish to influence. When social media is done well, it can attract a very large crowd, as it did for the Susan G. Komen Foundation Facebook fan page.

The key contributions of social media in the context of accelerating engagement are attraction and acceleration. Social media interactions can also provide value and options along your curve as well. Let's talk a bit about each of those items.

Attraction as a Key Contribution

Social media can draw a lot of people to you, your content, and your other supporters. The strategic question is whom do you wish to attract? Among the endless audience segments online, which are best aligned with the value you have to offer and are your best candidates not only for early engagement but also for progressing significantly far along your curve in short order? Where are they already gathering and interacting online? What can you do to get involved with them there and what can you offer to them to draw them to your main presence online and begin to build higher levels of engagement? All critical questions to answer.

Beyond or even in lieu of your own blogs and other social media, you can access the audiences of other social media outlets through sponsorship and advertising. There are many advertising networks, like Federated Media Publishing, who have brought dozens of blogs and other sites with niche audiences into their programs, allowing you to run highly focused ads for very specific audiences, usually at attractive prices. Organizations that pair a focused and valuable offering to a specific audience can draw high-value people to their offerings. High-value people are much more likely to accelerate along your engagement curve than others.

Acceleration as a Key Contribution

Social media efforts by your own staff and leadership can provide significant acceleration opportunities. One foundation that I worked with realized that the stories created at their highest levels of engagement often served as fuel for acceleration at the lower levels of engagement when retold to people at that stage. With this realized, they began working on creating video, audio, and text content that tells those stories, with clear calls to action, and sharing them through Facebook, blogs, and other channels they had developed. Enabling your leaders and other high-engagement individuals to tell their own stories in their own words via social media can be very powerful as well.

Membership directories that have been made more social as in LinkedIn and Facebook are also great platforms for creating acceleration. These tools can be used to make specific offers for next engagement actions with each participant as well as enabling people to share the story of their engagement with you. Always emphasize the importance of sharing these stories as well as making it easy to do so. This could be as simple as providing an option to update their status in a private social network with the news they have just renewed membership or registered for an event. It could also be as profound as posting a self-recorded video about what becoming a fellow of the organization means to them and thanking people in their life who helped them along the way.

Exercise: Maximize Your Free to Fee Strategy

Some thoughts to consider for your organization as you try to lead your constituents from free to fee may include the following:

- What electrical lines can you follow to discover new markets and customers?
- Who is the true buyer for what you are offering?
- Are you taking the time to build a relationship with your best prospects before going for the sale?
- How can you let your prospective customer, member, or volunteer experience what you have to offer before he or she has to buy?

CHAPTER 4

Data, Triggers, Stories, and Relationships: The Art and Science of Acceleration

I READ A REPORT RECENTLY about associations using email more frequently to market membership but seeing it as a less effective medium over time. I guarantee you that for organizations reporting those results, they are probably not attracting and gaining permission to market to their best prospective new members. Without a steady stream of new prospects giving permission to market to them, how do they expect to get new members via email marketing? It's like fishing in a pond where you have already caught and released every single fish but keep on hoping to find a new one.

It's pretty hard to accelerate engagement if you have no fuel for the engine.

Engagement Triggers

If you review your data, you should be able to identify segments of your customers who are more likely to buy product B if they have already purchased product A. Or they may have taken some other action you have captured that represents a meaningful change opening new opportunities for you to provide value. For example, your data may tell you that people who buy a guide to international widget marketing are much more likely to attend your international conference than others in your database. This insight allows you to target someone who just bought the guide to move to a higher level of engagement by attending the in-person conference. Crunching your data will likely reveal less obvious correlations that you can leverage to great effect. Using data, you can map out these connections and essentially develop an acceleration path comprised of a targeted chain of value that you can offer to relevant people.

My friend, Tom Breur, a master at turning data into dollars, wrote recently in his newsletter[1] about using automated triggers in your database to target customers for additional value when they have made a relevant purchase or taken some other step that indicates they are suitable. With Tom's permission, I have quoted the relevant passage below:

---

[1] www.xlntconsulting.com

Transactions Initiate Trigger-Based Marketing

Event-based marketing are actions that are triggered by changes in the customer's life. The term trigger-based marketing is also commonly used. We would consider an "event" a complex, multi-faceted occurrence in the customer's life. "Some" (unusual) trans-action will be a signal this event has taken place. For instance, a customer who has bought a house will subsequently change address. Or a (female) customer who gets married changes her name. A customer reports a stolen credit card, etcetera. Sometimes it is clear from the transaction which event has taken place (like in the case of a female changing her name after getting married), and sometimes it isn't.

If you understand the implications of an event to the customer's life, it can help you in servicing the customer better. Or possibly selling additional products. This can become a very efficient means of interacting if the campaign or dialogue follows automatically from the transaction that triggers identification of the event.

The key, as Tom points out, is to understand the changing needs reflected behind a particular action you record in your database and determine what targeted value you can offer to them. What are the most meaningful actions you currently capture? Based on that, what can you offer that is powerfully valuable to them given the new scenario they are in?

Data are not everything in accelerating engagement, however. At some point, it becomes necessary to transition to interpersonal relationships to move people effectively to the highest levels of engagement. I'll discuss that transition in more detail later in this chapter.

Case: Accelerating with Your Home Page

One of my clients, The Virginia Association of Realtors (VAR), baked in a lot of social media technology as well as improved content management when they re-launched their site in early 2010. Part of their strategy was to make it incredibly easy for their members to learn about news and events from the organization, part of the core value that VAR provides. The new home page is all about fulfilling that directive.

Here are the major sections of the home page and how they surface relevant action:

- **Visual Promo Box.** This box features rotating images that are related to the top stories and events and that the association wants to highlight. This is becoming a very common approach online and helps to create some visual interest while creating a great tool for guiding traffic.
- **Upcoming Meetings & Events.** This prominent section features programs put on by VAR, which is a big part of their work during the year.
- **News by Category.** Another key strategy is to get critical information to their members as quickly as possible. This section highlights that information and provides categorized tabs for sorting based on topic or issue.
- **MyVAR.** This is below the fold and features updates and content posted by the members' connections in VAR's social network on the site, surfacing what is new among their colleagues and friends.
- **Editor's Picks/Popular Stories.** This tool allows the staff to drive some content to the top while also highlighting what

content is being viewed the most. It is important to provide both types of featuring together because it allows VAR to drive content while also reflecting what people are viewing on their own.

These tools and techniques provide very prominent "next" actions to take from the home page that support creating engagement consistent with their mission and goals. Members and others can learn more about upcoming programs easily and some of them will become attendees, for example. This is a classic example of focusing your site to encourage people to move to the engagement opportunities you have to offer.

To measure success with this kind of approach you should set up conversion funnels in a web analytics tool, such as Google Analytics, that tracks how people flow from an initial page view through the various steps of completing a transaction or another important step on the site. Targeting conversion funnels at important engagement path milestones creates a highly relevant performance measurement tool that will help you to make decisions that actually result in new value for you and your website visitors.

Transition from Data-Driven Stage to Relationship-Driven Stage

An often-awkward transition for many organizations is recognizing when someone on your engagement curve transitions from the data-driven stage to the relationship-driven stage. Early engagement activities are largely driven by data and mass communication and interaction channels while the highest-value engagement opportunities are almost always relationship-driven, where personal interaction between staff and other volunteers or leaders in the organization drive people to the highest levels of engagement. Figure 4.1 shows where this transition point occurs for our hypothetical association.

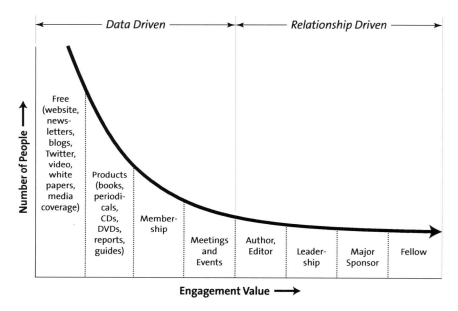

Figure 4.1: *The Data-Relationship Transition Point*

A lot of fundraisers and volunteer development people I have spoken and worked with indicate that the data-driven people (marketing) and the relationship-driven people (leadership development, high dollar fundraisers) aren't talking to each other enough. This leads to situations where someone who is personally ready to move along the engagement curve has to do some significant work on his or her part to make it happen. Think about your own organization. How do people tend to get noticed for those higher-level positions? It's usually because someone takes the initiative to introduce them to the right people so they can make it happen. I'll share a personal example of that with you.

I was sitting at a table at an annual meeting for a rather large association and got to chatting with another attendee I happened to sit next to. She shared with me all she had done with the association to date, which mostly consisted of going to conferences and local networking events, preparing for certification, and similar activities. She said what she really wanted to do next was get active on a committee or task force so she could contribute to the organization in a meaningful way (remember: meaningful to her). But she saw no clear path for how to make that happen from her experience with the organization to date.

I gave her the email address for the executive director of the association and said to drop him a note expressing her interest in doing more. She did, was appointed to a committee in short order and has since worked on a significant book project at the association. That's all it took to get someone over that transition from data-driven engagement to relationship-driven engagement.

Why in the world can't we do this with a regular process rather than relying on the kindness of strangers to do it for us? In fact, there is nothing stopping us from doing the work of increasing the rate at which people make that jump from data to relationship. Have you done any of the following?

- Developed a data-driven profile of the best prospects for high-level engagement?
- Identified those best prospects and sent them information on other opportunities?

- Reached out to those prospects to ask what they are interested in doing next with the organization through your current leadership and volunteers?
- Encouraged people you know well to constantly refer new talent and prospects (based on your profile) to you?
- Fully engaged with those outside your desired profiles as they find you?

As in almost every organizational endeavor, this transition from data to relationship can be put in place as a regular process. When I hear of organizations that have a hard time finding volunteers for activities, I always think that they simply need to take a deeper, more structured look at their current universe of constituents.

Building a Data-Driven Profile

Building a data-driven profile requires assessing the people who are in your highest tier of engagement. Look for characteristics they have in common that can be measured via your database. Are there specific programs, products, or services they use from your organization prior to moving to those higher levels? Are there certain demographic characteristics that correlate with this group? You can use these as elements of a profile to identify people in the data-driven sides of things as candidates for more personal interactions to move them to higher-level activities. The one danger to avoid is only looking at people fitting this profile. You must, of course, always be open to the serendipitous connection or person who takes the initiative him- or herself to move to a higher level.

I'll share a serendipitous and personal example with you about relationship-based engagement. I actually met my wife, Jennifer, in the elevator of my apartment building. I was in the elevator as the doors were about to close and saw her running to catch the door. I, being no dummy, held the door for the beautiful woman I'd never met before. In our short ride together we exchanged first names and learned enough to know we had both lived in the building for years without seeing each other. I got off at my floor, saying goodbye, thinking that she was very cute and too bad I probably wouldn't see her again. Shame on me! Jennifer, on the other hand, figured out which mailbox was mine based on my first name and the floor on which I exited the elevator. She put a note in my mailbox to invite me out for coffee. Now, we've been married for 11 years, have two kids, a cat, and a house together! I'm eternally grateful she took the initiative to keep us moving forward at that critical moment rather than leaving it to lucky circumstance again for our next encounter.

I'm afraid that too often we miss the opportunities to reach out to an individual and help him or her accelerate to the next step with our organizations, no matter the level at which he or she might be. These helping boosts can have a very long-term payoff well beyond the short-term value for everyone at the moment. We need both the regularity of procedures and processes to manage the transition from data to relationship as well as the ability and openness for the improvisational use of relationship at all levels to drive our organizations toward maximum engagement.

Stories and Legends Provide Fuel for Acceleration

The American Speech-Language-Hearing Foundation (ASHFoundation) uses stories to help move people along their engagement curve. Nancy Minghetti, the foundation's executive director, says that the students whose research they fund often become names in the field as their careers progress and some of them even create significant research results, made possible by the support provided to them by the foundation. These stories are powerful for the ASHFoundation with two important segments: donors and recipients.

For donors, these stories help to emphasize the tangible impact that their gifts to the foundation make possible. The stories can be used to entice first-time donors to give as well as to graduate current donors to higher levels of giving. For prospective recipients, the stories can help inspire more students to apply, giving the foundation a strong pool of talent to assess as they determine to whom to award grants.

In thinking about engagement as a process, Nancy and her staff are now exploring how to use social media as an avenue for recording and sharing these powerful stories with their target audience as well as making them integral parts of all the communication tools they use already.

Apple is another company that uses stories to fuel their growth. Apple has sold hundreds of millions of iPods since the company started offering the product in 2002. Many people who are now die-hard Apple buyers started with a mere iPod for their music. This opened a channel for them to consider themselves "Apple" people and become receptive to the stories told by Apple's marketing of how cool and hip owners of their products tend to be. (Full disclosure: I've bought a bunch of Apple stuff over the years.)

Figure 4.2 provides a visual depiction of how stories and legends generated at the top of the engagement curve can be used to fuel acceleration at the lower levels and up. If you listen to your

colleagues, members, customers, and volunteers, you will always hear
stories being told. We've always told stories. What's new here is using
them in a purposeful way to accelerate the creation of engagement
that you wish to create.

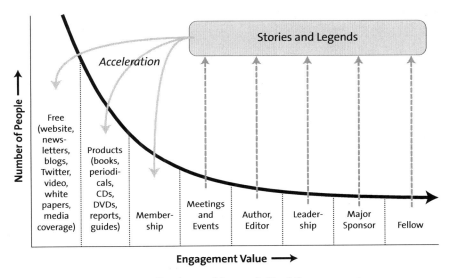

Figure 4.2: Stories and Legends Fuel Engagement

This is actually relatively easy to leverage, and your organization
is probably doing it in some fashion already. The real power comes
from identifying which stories tend to motivate people to increase
engagement with you and then work to gather, tell, record, and share
those stories so that the right people hear them.

In fact, the people who generate these stories often work quite
hard to spread them as well. ASAE's study of why people do (and
don't) join associations, found that "the more involved a person is
with a particular association, the more positive the rating becomes
for associations in general and the more likely they are to be a

promoter for the particular organization."[2] The study goes on to say that "word of mouth from a colleague is the number one way current members come to know about the association and the opportunity to join."[3] Clearly stories and legends drive engagement acceleration. Make sure your best stories are captured, shared, and leveraged to maximize the value you both receive from and give to your members, customers, and donors.

Exercise: Show Me the Money!

Explain to your team where the money comes from for your organization. This is often a critical oversight in a lot of organizations. Senior leadership is immersed in budget and cash flow on a daily basis. It's pretty easy to assume the rest of the staff is just as aware. They often are not.

Your team must know what provides the fuel for growing your organization, achieving your mission, and paying for their salaries. When they understand where the money comes from, it gives a much richer context for decisions and a framework for being more effective.

If you don't know where the money comes from, find out.

It is challenging to increase engagement, particularly engagement denominated in *dinero*, if the knowledge of where your revenue comes from is not widely known within the organization.

---

[2] *The Decision to Join*, Dalton and Dignam, ASAE, 2007, p 26.
[3] Ibid.

CHAPTER 5

Mind the Gap: Breaks in Your Curve Will Stop You Dead

SIGNIFICANT GAPS IN YOUR curve will slow down or even halt progression to higher-value engagement. Taking the example presented in the engagement acceleration curve in Chapter 2, if the association had no products to offer, it might have a harder time graduating people from free content to becoming actual paid members. Filling in that chasm would create a greater flow to higher-level activities, improving the association's revenue and contributions to its mission.

Figure 5.1 illustrates the problem of a gap in your offerings. Rather than accelerating down and out, people will become trapped in the gap because there is no easy path for them to continue to build engagement with you. If the Komen fan page did not have any specific next actions built into it, the organization would have wasted all of those potential supporters. Instead, they gave many opportunities to them to continue to build engagement after becoming a fan. When you consider lifetime value, this quickly adds up to a significant impact.

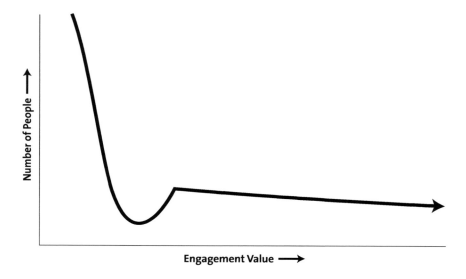

Figure 5.1: Mind the Gap

You will know the gaps in your curve largely by identifying programs, products, or services from which few people tend to progress. This illustrates a key lesson: Data are critical to both understanding your curve and enabling you to create targeted marketing to connect the various elements of it. Here are a few questions to ask of your data in order to find your gaps:

- What products, services, and events tend to be an end point for people engaging with us, where they rarely progress (or do so at a much lower rate) to higher value engagement opportunities?

- Are there specific segments that tend to get stuck at specific points on our engagement curve?
- Are certain activities always short of volunteers, limiting what can be achieved by them?

Questioning your data in this way will help you to identify those gaps in your engagement acceleration curve. Closing a gap in your curve can be the most strategically valuable act you take. This can unleash people pent up behind the gap and allow them to rush into greater engagement with the organization, maximizing value for everyone involved.

On the other hand, some organizations create gaps by design. Strict membership requirements will often stop people dead in their tracks if they do not qualify. In cases such as these, consider developing additional offerings of higher engagement value for people who cannot follow the main path. Many associations have a core membership who form a significant part of a market for specific industries. The vendors who serve these companies want to be engaged in the association but may not qualify for board service or other opportunities. In many cases, these people, key to the success of the industry as a whole, can be engaged in an industry advisory council that advises the board of directors from their unique perspective. This is an example of creating higher-value options for segments that may be barred from your main offerings.

Just because someone can't become a member (and there are often valid reasons for such requirements, as limiting as they are) doesn't mean you have to stop engaging with her at a certain point. It is only a zero-sum game if you choose to make it so.

Stopping Engagement Dead in Its Tracks

Seth Godin once wrote a blog post about upside versus downside, looking at how much effort you put into preventing bad things versus creating wonderful new things. He listed a hospital as one that does a lot of preventive work compared to the actual improvement of health. An art show, he says, is all about the upside and very little effort expended on prevention of the downside.

I had a visceral experience with a telecommunications company that not only spends way too much time on the downside, but it's actually their downside they are protecting rather than mine, their customer. My phone company had been pushing a new business phone plan for quite some time, calling me often and sending lots of mail. It actually looked like a reasonably good deal. I agreed to it when someone called me about it from the company. So far, so good.

Then they went into a very long process, recorded for later use, of the dire consequences of canceling this plan before the contract term is up. Fine, I said, let's keep going. After that call, I then received three separate calls from the company's reps again confirming (with recording) that I knew and accepted the early cancellation clause.

I'm now thinking: "Gee, this must be a pretty bad product if they are going to this length to make the contract length ironclad. I'm primed for failure at this point and the thing isn't even active yet." And then I received an email from them that misspelled my last name.

I know your organization is not this bad, unless you are working with a telecommunications company perhaps. But how much are you doing to wow your new customers? They just invested money with you in exchange for value. Per Seth's point, the faster and greater you can deliver value to them on the upside, the better they will appreciate the investment they just made and become predisposed to loving your product or service. This is one key to acceleration: Each interaction must deliver value and entice the person to want to move to higher levels of value with you sooner or later.

After this experience, I'm about as eager to sign up for a new service from this company as I am to get a root canal. I'll do it only when I desperately need it and have no other option. That is not a great business model.

The lesson to keep in mind here is that a poor experience during engagement can essentially create gaps in your acceleration curve. Why move forward with this organization if they just disappointed you so much? This is another factor to explore, especially if the data show you have a gap forming after one particular event or product, but the jump to the next level is not that great, on paper at least. Poor customer service very well may create that gap by driving people away from you.

As you might guess, fantastic customer service experiences will tend to accelerate engagement overall. You want people thinking, "That was so great, I can't wait to come back for more!"

How Zappos Fills Gaps

Zappos, an online shoe retailer recently acquired by Amazon, does not tolerate gaps in their engagement curve. I identified 22 potential next actions you can take on a product page for a pair of Clarks shoes. These are just in the main content area, without regard to the navigational options around the periphery of the page:

• Return to browsing (previous page)

- Jump to customer reviews
- See all products from Clarks
- Select color, size, and width
- Add to cart (in shocking orange)
- See shipping options
- Add to my favorites
- See more images of the shoes
- View available colors
- Copy a short link to the page
- Tell a friend
- Share page via social media sites
- Share in a blog (copy code)
- View a video description of the product
- Write a review
- See a glossary of terms used by Zappos
- Call Zappos for help
- Browse related products
- Read more reviews
- Add Clarks brand to my favorites
- Notification via email of new styles from Clarks
- Submit a video testimonial

Every single one of these actions contributes to accelerating Zappos' business goals. They help visitors learn about the product, buy it, review it, and share with others. They have identified any potential gap between someone viewing a product and that person buying that product. Are you doing half as much to accelerate your own engagement opportunities?

Exercise: What One Gap Can You Close Immediately?

Here is a way to close a single gap rather quickly.

Call your team together and identify several gaps in your engagement acceleration curve. As a group or separate teams, come up with at least three ideas for how you can close each gap, including both short- and long-term solutions.

Now go through the list of ideas and identify which one requires the least amount of time and resources to implement, yet is likely to have a significant impact in helping to bridge a critical engagement gap. Take that item and identify the first five steps that must happen to put it into effect and assign them to people in the room with deadlines to achieve them.

It's really that simple and can have a powerful impact on the value you are delivering to your members and other constituents. The best organizations do this as a regular process. Try it a few times yourself and then make it routine in a way that is both sustainable and effective for your culture and resources.

Zap the Sacred Zombie Cows: Or the Art of the Stop

NNOVATION, CREATING GREATER VALUE with new or existing
resources, is a critical element of the engagement acceleration
process. What drew people to you five years ago may only be
attracting flies today! Innovating engagement opportunities is
absolutely required as a long-term activity to keep your organization
healthy, vibrant, and growing. This is pretty obvious to most people
today, given our recent history, but a lot of executives effectively tie
one hand behind their back in the innovation department. Here's why.

Many organizations innovate through growth. As membership
increases or non-dues revenue goes up, they now have more
resources with which to start new initiatives. Innovating new
value is much easier for leaders when you have a healthy growing

organization. You can just put that new money to work and let the rest of things carry on, avoiding tough conversations and decisions.

The challenge comes when that growth stops or reverses, something many have become familiar with over the past few years. If the only way your organization can innovate is through growth, then you now face a serious problem: Just when you need to be the most nimble, you are actually at your least flexible.

This is what I call the Growth Trap: Relying only on growth for change traps you in the status quo when that growth goes away. Thus, being able to stop doing things not only makes for a more responsive organization; it is an existential necessity in tough times.

If your organization has come through the depths of the recession, you have probably learned how to stop doing things that are no longer of value, allowing you to reallocate those resources. Don't forget this precious skill once your revenues are back on the upswing. It will continue to serve you well in good times and will make it much easier for you to weather the inevitable downturns when they come.

Have You Killed Your Sacred Zombie Cow Today?

You must kill your sacred zombie cow if you want your organization to survive and thrive. Allow me to explain.

Mark Parker, CEO of Nike, said in an interview that his top priority is making sure his company edits, that it removes products and ideas of low quality and value. Parker said that Steve Jobs once told him that Nike is a great company but it would be better if they stopped making "crap."

As Parker implicitly admitted in the interview, it is hard to stop making crap even if you already produce some of the best products in your industry. If it were easy, Parker wouldn't care about it.

The problem with crap is that it is too easy to make. Crap keeps people busy. We've always made crap! But crap gets in the way of making the remarkable, the insanely valuable, the things for which you are the best.

Thus the focus on editing at Nike.

Enter the sacred zombie cow. Sacred zombie cows are the purest manifestation of crap within an organization. These are programs, products, and services that are a net negative to the company and yet are incredibly hard to kill. They no longer have a strong sponsor on the scene but still they shamble along, eating up resources. People tend to walk around sacred zombie cows like they are just a piece of furniture, ignoring how utterly dangerous they are.

Peter Drucker, the godfather of business strategy, said that the most innovative companies are those that are ruthless about stopping things. They maniacally root out and destroy sacred zombie cows, like a Van Helsing in Dockers.

Why are these highly innovative companies so focused on the art of the stop? Because it frees up resources that can be invested to develop new products, services, and programs. It is that simple.

Innovation solely through growth is inherently unsustainable. At some point all organizations hit a plateau. Those that never bothered to learn how to stop something go from radical growth to radical stagnation.

If you've been editing out the sacred zombie cows all along, then the chances of hitting a plateau are less, and when you do hit one, you have the ability to change at the precise moment that you need to.

Find your sacred zombie cow. Turn around; it's right behind you. Now drive a stake through its heart. Or defenestrate it. Or give it away to another company! Do what you must to get it out and gone forever. Even if you are the one who turned it loose in the first place.

Killing sacred zombie cows is an act of optimism. It frees your organization to focus on excellence. More personally, it just might unleash a creative burst that takes you to a new level of achievement.

I commissioned Hugh MacLeod to draw this cartoon to illustrate the concept of sacred zombie cows in the fun way that only Hugh can. You can download this "cube grenade" from www.orgpreneur.com and print it out for your own office wall or to serve as inspiration in your next staff or board meeting.

How to Track Sacred Zombie Cows in the Wilds of Your Organization

Here are the worst signs of a sacred zombie cow in your organization. If you notice more than one of these with a particular program, product, service, or process, then you may have a zombie on your hands.

- Low or decreasing revenue and profits
- Declining participation
- No one will admit to owning it, even if that person is the one running it!
- Nobody gets excited about it or suggests new ideas for how to make it better
- No one defends it but no one ever suggests getting rid of it

Five Techniques for Slaying Your Zombie Cow

There are five techniques that I can suggest for slaying your zombie cow. They are

1. **Just stop it!** Bob Newhart did a hilarious skit[1] where he played a therapist listening to his patient's fear of being buried alive in a box. When the patient asked what she should do, Bob yelled, "Stop it!" at the top of his lungs. Many times we can simply just stop the program or service or product that is no longer producing value. Ask yourself, would anyone notice if we stopped it? If not, this might be worth a shot as the simplest solution.

---

[1] http://www.youtube.com/watch?v=T1g3ENYxg9k

2. **Make the case to stop it.** This is like making a business case for starting a new product or service except you are using it for creating a case to do away with the program instead. Run the numbers. Look at the overhead. Identify opportunities lost because these resources are tied up. Then make the case to whoever needs to approve the change.

3. **Merge it with something else.** Can the program be merged or melded with something else, in essence granting those resources to a more successful program? This is a more subtle approach that achieves the same effect as ending the program without actually ending it and can be useful when support for outright killing of the zombie can't be mustered.

4. **Give it away to some other organization.** This is the one no one ever thinks of but often solves the problem quite nicely. Give it away! Find some organization or group that actually values this shambling beast and give it to them. Why not?

5. **Put a good crisis to work.** I gave a speech to a room full of Chamber of Commerce executives during the depths of the market crash in 2009. Not a fun time for most of them! When I asked if anyone had killed off a sacred zombie cow program, two people shared that their chambers had done away with golf tournaments that had been stagnating for a long time and that everyone, including the golfers, was simply going through the motions to complete. They canceled them, applied those resources to more productive areas, and no one complained. This is radical! Golf tournaments are what chambers *do*! As Machiavelli advises, "Never waste the opportunities offered by

a good crisis." Sometimes that's what it takes to kill off sacred zombie cows. Don't be afraid to use them!

Exercise: Turning Stopping into a Process Rather than an Event

Ultimately, the slaying of sacred zombie cows should be a process that you engage in on a regular basis. Growth allows new resources for investment, but becoming great at the art of the stop allows you to generate free resources no matter whether you are growing, treading water, or even in decline. It is a critical skill for resiliency in the face of any environment.

Here are a few methods you can use to turn stopping into a process for your team or organization:

- **Stopping Begins at the Start.** When planning a new product, service, or initiative, identify the conditions or results that indicate you should stop doing it. We often focus on success metrics, with good reason, but putting some thought into what failure looks like and drawing a line where you'll call it a day can be very beneficial as well. This avoids having to draw that line at a time when it's a much more loaded question.

- **Create a Watch List.** Once a quarter, develop a watch list of items that should be considered for elimination. Perhaps you go ahead and give the axe now if it's a clear case. For borderline cases, leave them on the list and check in again at the next quarter and see if they have improved, declined, or held steady. Items that are back to health can be taken off the list while any that linger too long can finally be eliminated. The failure metrics mentioned above are invaluable for this kind of exercise as well.

- **Ask Your Board or Senior Executives.** Once a year ask your top leadership to identify at least one thing that the organization can stop today because it no longer adds value. We are always asking leadership what new things we should do but often a greater contribution is to help definitively cut some things in order to free up resources for future growth.

Go out there and stop something!

CHAPTER 7

How to Map Your Curve: From Islands to Acceleration

O NE OF THE CORE values of mapping out an engagement acceleration curve is that it helps you to bridge your disparate offerings with intent, moving people effectively from one to another and maximizing the total impact you create in the world in pursuit of your mission. It is also critical for helping you to identify gaps in your curve that need to be filled in order to be successful. This chapter gives you some tips and ideas on how to map out your curve in order to achieve maximum engagement. (For more information about accelerating engagement with your constituents see Appendix A: The Big List of Engagement Ideas and Their Values.)

Diagnosing Your Own Engagement Performance

A key first step in this process is to diagnose your current engagement performance. This knowledge will help you know if you are doing great, need some adjustment, or have major rework and reengineering ahead of you.

I've developed a handy double-axis chart (see Figure 7.1) that you can use with your staff, executive team, and leadership to quickly identify where your organization is in terms of engagement. The vertical axis represents your ability to accelerate engagement, moving people effectively among all the offerings you have. This ranges from weak at the bottom of the axis to strong at the top. The horizontal axis represents the engagement opportunities that you currently offer, where people can exchange time and/or money with you in exchange for value. This axis ranges from Few/Uniform on the left, where you only have a few offerings, to Many/Diverse, where you offer a wide array of engagement opportunities.

I'll discuss the four quadrants this chart forms later in this chapter but first I want to address the precision of knowledge you need in order to put this chart into use. For early efforts, going with your gut is usually good enough. If you are being honest, most organizations know if you offer a diverse array of engagement opportunities or if you are relatively narrow. Likewise, you probably have a good idea at how good a job you do at moving people among these options. So, don't be afraid to use the knowledge and experience of those in the room for your initial diagnosis. Once you have plotted where you are and where you need to go, you can go back and verify by looking at your actual data before making and implementing substantial plans for change. It's vastly more important to have this conversation *now* based on imperfect knowledge, than it is to wait until you have perfect knowledge. In this world, perfect knowledge doesn't exist, even with all the tools and data at our fingertips.

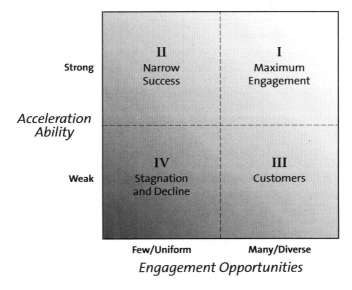

Figure 7.1: Assessing Organizational Engagement

Let's take a look at each of the quadrants formed in this chart and their associated characteristics.

- **Quadrant I: Maximum Engagement Zone.** Quadrant I is the goal for most organizations. You have a diverse array of offerings and are excellent at moving people among them. I call this the Maximum Engagement Zone where you are rapidly progressing people to higher levels of engagement through all the offerings you provide.

- **Quadrant II: Narrow Success Zone.** Quadrant II is where a lot of organizations live for a long time. I call this the Narrow

Success Zone since you are effectively engaging people but you are doing so only with a small set of products, services, and activities. This can actually work well from a financial standpoint and even for your mission but it does create some risk because you are so concentrated in what you offer. Having a wider array of offerings creates less reliance on any single program, which makes the organization much more resilient when faced with change. This is why I think that Quadrant I is preferable to Quadrant II. That said, it is a valid strategic choice to remain narrow so long as you have weighed the strategic risks in doing so and are ready to rapidly change when needed.

- **Quadrant III: Spread Too Thin Zone.** In Quadrant III you have a lot of offerings but you are not moving people through and among them effectively. This might show a lack of marketing, poor database infrastructure, not enough new prospects entering the organization, too many sacred zombie cows, among other potential causes. Organizations in this zone will have a lot of unprofitable offerings or barely break even offerings and not enough volunteers for leadership roles. Once the cause of this status is identified, you can then make changes to either narrow down and go to Quadrant II or beef up your acceleration ability and move to Quadrant I. You know which one I recommend! (Hint: It matches the title of this book!)

- **Quadrant IV: Stagnation and Decline.** Ah, the dreaded Quadrant IV. This is where organizations go to die. There are few offerings of any relevancy to your target markets and poor ability to engage people with them. Drastic action is necessary if leadership wants to turn this situation around with any hope for success, starting with assessing why the organization should continue to exist at all. If no good reason is found, perhaps it's time to wind it down and move on. Sometimes *you* are the sacred zombie cow! If you commit to moving out of this space, make sure you have a strongly committed core of supporters who all agree on why it matters to save the organization. You'll need nothing less.

You should also use this device to assess your performance after implementing changes to fill gaps and accelerate engagement within your organization. Have you moved out of your current quadrant to your desired target? Are you successfully holding position in Quadrant I? What more do you need to do to stay there? You get the idea.

The Six Steps to Mapping Out your Engagement Acceleration Curve

Here is your quick guide to mapping out your engagement curve once you have diagnosed your current situation.

1. Conduct an engagement inventory, listing all the options for engaging with your organization in terms of time and money. Website, webinar, book, annual meetings, donor, sponsor, and committee member are all examples of engagement.
2. Place each major item, or grouping of similar activities or products, onto an index card.

3. Order the cards on a table or wall, sorting by increasing levels of engagement and the number of people you estimate are involved in each.

4. Use this layout to identify where you have great strengths in engagement or significant gaps that must be overcome.

5. Add new cards of a different color to indicate where you will add items to cover gaps or otherwise bolster a certain area.

6. Flag existing cards that you may remove to reduce redundancies or eliminate sacred zombie cows that are no longer providing value.

And that's about it! Asking and answering critical questions to generate and sort these lists is what generates the value here.

Management by Lego: Make Sure Your Pieces Snap Together

Every engagement opportunity in your curve needs two things: engagement feeders and engagement targets.

Engagement feeders are those products, services, activities, and actions that feed into an engagement opportunity. They create and/or channel demand for something else. Engagement targets are those engagement opportunities that the current action, product, or service is designed to feed people into.

Lego building blocks, the universal toy of childhood in much of the world, have bumps on top and sockets on the bottom. They snap together with a satisfying click. Many of your engagement offerings must do the same with each other, pairing feeders with targets, in an ever-increasing chain of engagement value.

In the 1990s, I helped develop an international membership section for a large business association. One year, we decided to add in an international certificate seminar program. We identified many feeders from existing activities (membership, product purchases, event attendance) that would serve as a natural foundation for this program to build upon. Later on, this successful program eventually led to develop of a formal certification program for individuals in this subject area, providing a target for this program to feed into.

Thinking of your programs, products, and services as part of an integrated process of engagement, snapping together like Lego blocks, makes for a much easier time in marketing and generating action.

How to Identify Your Potential Breakout Successes

Get out a piece of paper and draw three intersecting circles, a classic Venn diagram. Label one Organization, the second You, and the third Boss/Team.

Each of these circles represents excitement. For the organization, this includes the things that senior executives, the Board, or the strategy du jour have identified as highly important. The circle for You contains the things that you are personally excited to work on or develop. Finally, the third circle covers those items that your team and/or your boss are personally invested in and will to go the extra mile for success.

That intersection is your breakout zone, where a runaway success is possible. These projects, products, or programs should receive a lot of your attention because you have the greatest chance to create tremendous impact with that much aligned focus.

This is a great conversation to have as a group or team as well. Jointly identify what is in that intersection and how you can really make a difference with it.

Comparing Time and Money as Engagement

When planning new items for your engagement acceleration curve (or evaluating existing ones), it's helpful to get a handle on the time and money investment they require of the people you are engaging with. We can also flip this question and use it to consider the people themselves and the market segments they represent.

Figure 7.2 below illustrates a comparison between money and time investments, contrasting low options and high options for both dimensions. Items that are low on the money axis might be free or relatively low-cost compared to your other offerings. Activities requiring a high amount of time commitment are represented at the high end of the time axis on this chart. The interesting stuff happens at the intersections of these two dimensions.

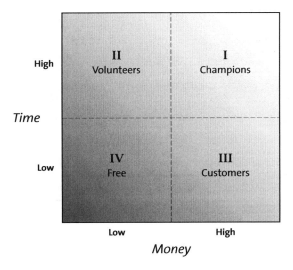

Figure 7.2: Comparing Time and Money as Engagement

- **Quadrant IV: Free.** This quadrant represents both a low-time and a low-money investment in exchange for some form of value. When you plan your offerings in this quadrant, they should have a relatively low cost to develop and deliver because they will be offered to the largest number of people. This corresponds to the far left of the engagement acceleration curve. Many people new to your organization will start out here. Questions to consider of this quadrant include
  - What do we have to offer for free that will scale well *and* attract our best prospects?
  - What will the offerings in this section lead to next on our curve?
  - Do we have too many offerings here, starving resources for other sections?

– Do we have too little to offer for a low- or no-cost and
a small time investment? Are we missing out on people
we could have pulled closer to us by not having sufficient
value in this quadrant?

• **Quadrant III: Customers.** This quadrant represents simple
customers or donors, those who give you money in exchange
for value (products/services or supporting a cause they care
about) but who otherwise give very little time to the organization. In the association world, these folks are often referred
to as "check book" members, in that their sole significant
interaction with the organization is to cut a check to pay their
membership dues in exchange for the benefits of membership.
While it's tempting to consider these folks as failed opportunities for higher engagement, they are often quite profitable to
serve. The key, as I emphasize throughout this book, is to learn
the signs of someone who is ready to move to a new level with
you in terms of engagement and then help them to do so. Some
questions to consider with this quadrant include
  – Do we offer a wide array of opportunities to invest money
  with the organization or do we rely on one or two big
  programs?
  – Is there a range of investment opportunities from
  relatively low money to high money in this quadrant?
  – Are the offerings here profitable? This is where the health
  of the organization's bottom line will be determined.
  – For donations, are we raising enough money to fuel
  our activities related to achieving our mission? Are we

purposely moving people further into this quadrant at higher giving levels?

- **Quadrant II: Volunteers.** This quadrant represents a high level of time investment with relatively low money involved. I label this section "volunteers," which is the primary activity reflected by those in this quadrant. Volunteering is rapidly evolving in today's wired (and wireless) world and should now be expanded to include both those in traditional roles and those who help spread the word about your organization and mission online. It can also include those who are part of working committees and boards, help run events, make fundraising calls, and give time to other activities to help support the cause or field. For professional societies, speakers and authors are a significant component of this sector. Some questions to consider in this quadrant include

  – Do we have enough people to fulfill all the volunteer roles available?

  – Do we have more people than volunteer opportunities?

  – Is our online content easily and actively shared via social media channels? Are we cultivating relationships with those online champions for us, providing them "insider" information and access?

  – Are we moving people from this quadrant toward money-related activities, and vice versa, with intent?

- **Quadrant I: Champions.** Finally, this quadrant represents those who invest a significant amount of money and time with the organization. These are your engagement champions who make significant investments along both dimensions. This could be the board member who is also a major donor and chief rainmaker. It could be someone who has served on committees and task forces for years and buys everything the organization has to offer when it comes out. You get the idea and can probably name many of these folks off the top of your head. Questions to consider here include

- Have you developed a profile to identify the best candidates for Quadrant I?
- Are you regularly reviewing your top people in Quadrant II and Quadrant III and seeing how you can move them to Quadrant I?
- Are you capturing the stories generated by your top people in this section and using them to inspire and activate those in other quadrants?
- How large a contribution to your mission and bottom line does this quadrant make to the overall organization?

The interesting thing about this chart is that you need people in all four quadrants at all times. Use Quadrant IV to draw new people to you. Graduate those folks to Quadrant II and Quadrant III and then mark your all-star candidates to go to Quadrant I and become your maximum engagement champions.

The Two Tremendous Advantages NPOs Have Over Business

Nonprofit organizations (NPOs) of all types typically have two advantages over for-profit competitors: trust and data.

NPOs are trusted more than businesses quite often. The trust comes from being a mission-focused organization as well as knowing that profits are reinvested to support the mission rather than paid out to owners or shareholders.

Many organizations also have a tremendous amount of data about their market already on hand. You know who the big givers are, you know who is in your profession, and you know who comes to more meetings and events than others. These data are priceless.

Businesses would give a lot to have the same advantages.

Use the trust you have been given to offer value to your members, volunteers, donors, and others. Use those data to make highly relevant offers and communications to these same people. For example, I know one association that simply sent relevant session information to specific segments when marketing early registration for the group's annual meeting. This simple change, telling people about the sessions most relevant to them rather than bombing the whole program out to them, helped the association to hit their registration targets three months earlier than they ever had before. Wow! The opportunities are endless if you make the effort to learn from and use your data, just like the big for-profit companies do.

Fulfilling your mission as an NPO doesn't mean you have to be a doormat. Embrace your advantages! Put them to work. You owe it to your mission and your constituents.

Products Must Be Profitable

Products must be profitable in terms of engagement. Engagement profit can be measured by revenue but also by the value of the time and involvement the person invests with the product. Additional engagement value can be measured by the product serving as a loss leader for other more valuable engagement opportunities. Let's take the new model of micro-pricing and see how it appears as a good candidate for inclusion in any curve but actually is quite challenging to do successfully.

I work with a lot of membership organizations and the idea of micro-payments is often very appealing to their leaders. They provide a very low price point on some products which they can point to when members complain about overall prices of products. It's also quite trendy, with high-profile examples like Kiva.com leading the way with their business model for microlending, connecting individual investors with those who could benefit from a very small loan.

Let's take a look at the math for a hypothetical association. Let's say it is a scientific society with 20,000 members who pay $399 a year to join. We'll use them as our pre-qualified base of prospects for a micro-payment product.

Evernote, the very popular note-taking application that works on almost anything with a chip and a screen, recently shared some stats. Shortly after the society started up, about 1 percent of its free users converted to paying customers.

If we take a micro-priced product at $1 and 1 percent of our hypothetical base makes the purchase, then you end up with this:

$$(20,000 \times 1\%) \times \$1 = \$200$$

Compare that revenue to what the society gets in membership dues:

$$20,000 \times \$399 = \$7,980,000$$

The organization will literally waste more in jammed paper in their printers than they would make on this single micro-priced product. This is before taking into account the costs of producing the product and implementing micro-payments, online access, etc. Having a single staff meeting to discuss this product already puts it in the hole!

This association would need a base market of about 2 million people to make the revenue even slightly interesting with these assumptions. They still need a lot more people in that market even if you bump up the price and the conversion rate. In terms of the engagement acceleration curve, you would need to have an absolutely huge market feeding into the far left of the curve in order to be able to move enough of them to a micro-priced product to actually make a profit. The one exception to this would be if offering the product itself met some political or policy need of great value to the organization. Even so, it would need to be a pretty hefty return in that area for it to be worthwhile.

One lesson to draw from this about pricing in general is that it is a lot easier to earn significant profit by offering a high-price, high-margin product and service to a relatively small market than it is to go full retail selling low-priced, low-margin products to millions of people.

Case: Making Money with *BusinessWeek*

Bloomberg L.P., which recently agreed to acquire *BusinessWeek* from McGraw Hill Companies, has announced some details of its plans for the venerable publication, according to *Mediaweek*. These include expanding content and adding greater international focus. They also intend to begin charging for content online.

The relevant quote from the news story: "As for the Web, Bloomberg plans to keep most of its content free while creating deep, vertical content areas that paying users could access for roughly $100 a year."

This shows a clear strategy of attracting a broad audience with freely available content and then converting a portion of that group into paid subscribers who value deep content in well-defined areas. This is a strategy that I think can work long term. People have always paid for content when they have seen the value. Perceptions of value are changing rapidly with experience on the web, which is causing the massive changes that the publishing industry is trying to survive.

In short, don't believe those who say paid content is a dead model; it is not. It simply has to be placed into the right strategic context for today's world rather than that of 10 years ago. *BusinessWeek* will be one to watch to see how they do.

Watch How Others Reinvent Your Own Business Model

Four internet marketers and social media business model gurus got together and launched a membership site earlier this year: Third Tribe Marketing.

In exchange for a monthly fee of $49, you get access to a full archive of their past content plus several new educational pieces each month, all focused on how to build online businesses. They also have a forum for members to interact and mutually coach each other in applying the techniques from the educational content.

The site launched with 2,000 members at an early promotional rate of $25 a month. Not bad.

Why this worked:
- The joint authors have very strong brands with their target market.
- They used technology to make it easy to generate, publish, and distribute content.
- Their members provide additional value via forums.
- Their target audience is more than willing to spend and learn online.
- It is offered at a relatively low monthly price point.
- They turn their members into affiliates, who market the program and get paid for conversions.
- And last, but not least, the content they offer is highly valued by their members.

The content they are offering is primarily based on recorded interviews and discussions with simple action planning tips in a document. This kind of content is not hard to create, quite frankly. This business model has profound potential for any traditional membership organization.

Information Wants to Be Expensive

In a 1984 presentation, Steward Brand famously declared that information wants to be free. He was referring to how, even in the 1980s, the cost to transmit and receive information was rapidly approaching zero. Charging for access to random information thus becomes very hard to sustain when the cost of doing so is perceived as essentially zero by most people. This is what the internet and the web have wrought to industry after industry. As of this writing, video rental outfit Blockbuster is publicly discussing bankruptcy. After annoying generations with late fees, other companies have found a superior way to deliver the same information (video entertainment) at a lower cost.

What most people fail to quote along with that bit is that Brand also said that information wants to be expensive, "The right information in the right place just changes your life." Information delivered to the right person at the right time for their highest need is of tremendous value to the recipient. The cost of storing, publishing, or delivering that information is of no importance to them.

This is why information products must be embedded in a context that maximizes their value if you want to maximize what you can charge for it. That valuable context can be provided by several factors. Among them are

- **Immediacy.** I have a problem right now and I'll pay well for the perfect information to solve to it quickly without having to do a bunch of research.

- **Importance.** The opportunity or problem at hand is so significant that I'm willing to pay well for information to help me make decisions and move forward.

- **Authority.** I trust the source of this information more than any other and am willing to pay a premium for information from this source because I don't have to worry about the quality or authenticity of the material. You might also think of this dimension as the brand of the publisher or provider.

The more of those three factors, and the greater the degree of each, that you can incorporate into your offerings, the better response you will have. I'll provide an example from the publisher of this book, ASAE, to illustrate how it works.

In 2003, the U.S. Congress passed CAN-SPAM, which was subsequently signed into law by President George W. Bush, a law that set national standards for sending commercial email and put the Federal Trade Commission in charge of enforcement. Associations were already tremendous senders of emails to their members and other constituents at that point, and this law had potentially huge impact in penalties if you broke the rules. ASAE held a series of in-person and online events to bring people up to speed on the law, regulations, and enforcement as it all developed over the course of a couple of years. These programs were well attended and often sold out. ASAE combined all three elements, immediacy, importance, and authority, to create highly compelling offerings that were both free and for a fee.

Evaluate each of your offerings along these three dimensions. If you are seeing poor uptake for a new product, the chances are you need to place it into a higher-value context by better positioning it along these dimensions in marketing and advertising or perhaps having to revamp the content to better fit a more compelling context. High-value context makes your buyers want information to be expensive, or at least worthy of a higher investment to have access to it.

Exercise: How to Accelerate People Along the Curve

We have discussed various approaches and techniques for accelerating people along your engagement path throughout the book. I want to revisit a few of those and provide some other techniques in a brief summary. Consider how you can use one or more of these approaches for each of your engagement opportunities in order to move people along quickly and smoothly.

- **Troll the Social Web:** Identify blogs, social networks, forums, and other places online where your best prospective members, donors, participants, and others congregate and interact. Ideally these places are relevant to the value you offer as well. Buy advertising, post content, partner with the publishers, and do whatever you can to get your organization in front of them there and entice them to one of your sites.

- **Get an Email Address:** When those new people come to you via your trolling online or simply natural search results or links, offer something of value in exchange for an email address. Newsletter, free eBook, anything that gives you permission to put messages in front of this person on a regular basis. Then provide offers to them periodically that are the logical next step on your curve.

- **Segment Communication and Offers:** People expect tailored information these days and have always responded more effectively to it. Never blast a message to all if it contains important actions you wish people to take. Always place those actions into the context of why it is so powerfully in their own self interest to do it that they almost don't have to think about it before taking action.

- **What is the Best Input for this Opportunity?** For any given engagement opportunity, consider what the best input is for it. What products, services, experiences, or other behavior can you identify to make someone a great prospect for this offer? Create your list based on that and offer it to them!

- **What is the Best Output for this Opportunity?** For people who are thrilled with a current opportunity, what is the next set of offers that are the best candidates for them to get even more value from the organization or to take their contribution to your mission even higher? Make those offers on a regular basis. This and the prior tip can be automated to a great extent in the data-driven phase of your curve.

- **Recognize and Leverage the Data/Relationship Transition:** As discussed earlier, there is a transition point where people shift from mass-communication and data-driven engagement to relationship-based engagement growth. Make sure you know where that point is for you and that you facilitate the transition for as many people as possible.

- **Create a Growth Path for the Relationship Stage:** Large corporations often develop specific career paths for high-potential employees, the future leaders of the company. They move these people around the world in a variety of roles and operations in order to give them the best chance to fully develop themselves and their ultimate contribution to the organization. Do the same thing for your high-potential

volunteers, donors, and participants. Create a custom path
for them and talk to them about how they can grow with the
organization and what the options are. Find out what they are
interested in and see how you can develop those opportunities
for them.

Apply the above techniques consistently over time and watch your
constituents fly down the engagement curve for your organization.

CHAPTER 8

Riding the Curve: From Plan to Action

I CLOSE OUT THE BOOK with some observations on how to take your engagement plan and make it a reality. No strategy ever failed on the white board: It's when things see the light of day and begin to be put to work that they can fall apart. This chapter is all about maximizing your chances of success at achieving maximum engagement. (See Appendix A: The Big List of Engagement Ideas and Their Values for ideas on creating engagement in terms of time and money.)

The Most Common Engagement Challenges

There are four very common challenges in creating and accelerating engagement. I list them below along with what actions are required to resolve them.

1. The organization has no clear engagement progression path. A lot of organizations have run on momentum, doing the programs and services they have always provided without a lot of consideration for how to move people among them with intent or whether there are gaps. Organizational silos can also prevent viewing engagement as an encompassing process across the organization, also decreasing the speed at which people move across those channels. In facing this situation, a great first step is to educate leadership and the senior team about engagement and the importance of having an engagement strategy for the entire organization based on the acceleration curve. (Giving them all copies of this book would be a good first step!) Use the engagement acceleration curve to see how your offerings are related to each other and use it as a guide to point out where bridges between your internal silos must be built. Great engagement paths provide a full spectrum of engagement opportunities, from viewing web pages to serving as your top leadership and supporters. This path should be relatively smooth, without any significant jumps in value that would require significant leaps of faith by the people you wish to engage. Finally, your organization must apply technology, communication, marketing, and personal relationships to the curve in order to accelerate people along the path.

2. The organization has significant engagement gaps requiring leaps that are too far for most people to progress easily to the next level with you. This is actually a great situation to encounter because it provides an opportunity to have a rather large impact in short order. Filling gaps can unleash pent-up engagement, allowing many people to progress to higher levels of engagement with you. Refer back to Chapter 5 for more on this.

3. Engagement increases over time but it is too slow. Another common scenario is that you have a pretty good set of escalating engagement options in place, yet the progression through them is lacking alacrity. Chapter 4 went in depth into techniques for creating acceleration. This is another great scenario, in that you have the basics in place and simply need to use technology, marketing, communication, and relationships to move people along.

4. The organization lacks resiliency when formerly productive engagement activities stop performing, leading to growing gaps and loss of acceleration. This was really what the whole sacred zombie cow concept was about, as we discussed in Chapter 6. If you cannot eliminate things that are no longer delivering value, then you'll be hard pressed to add new ones that do. This is probably the single greatest thing you can do to create a resilient organization: Get in the business of stopping things as well as starting. This is a notoriously tough thing for nonprofit organizations to do effectively but it is possible!

Break Out of the Zero Sum Game Trap

When wrestling with the conflicting pressures to increase revenue while pricing products lower, the best approach is freeing yourself from the zero-sum game paradigm. Zero-sum games come from the field of game theory, which was often used to explain how nation states compete with each other. In zero-sum games, if one party gains, the other must by rule lose an equal or greater amount. By design it is tough for everyone in a zero-sum system to benefit.

Zero-sum thinking prevents organizations from growing engagement a lot of time. The following questions are examples of zero-sum thinking:

- Should we move resources from our members-only area to the public section, making them free?
- Should we offer $20 audio download products or $200?
- Should we break out some benefits currently provided as part of membership and charge separately for them?

That last one is especially dangerous. This is precisely what the airlines are doing to make up for the fact that many of them have positioned themselves so they can't be profitable based on what they charge for the actual ticket. In the association world, this used to be referred to as bundling or unbundling of products and services: very zero-sum thinking that limits your organization's potential.

The happy truth is, however, that most of us are not actually operating in zero-sum systems! If you are, it is usually because of choice or not perceiving the other paths available to you.

The single greatest thing is to drop the word "or" from your vocabulary and start using "and" much more often. The debate isn't between free or members-only content; it's about what free content you should offer to attract more members to benefit from that rich trove of members-only resources!

Bridging Silos

Breaking down silos is a frequent organizational mantra. However, if taken to the extreme, you end up with a pile of rubble and scavengers making off with your grain.

The simple truth of the matter is that no organization can be made perfect, they all have their inefficiencies, politics, and barriers. Sometimes the more effective approach is to bridge silos rather than break them down. You are much less likely to bring the whole edifice down on your head if you focus on punching strategic holes in the towers and connecting them rather than trying to take on the entire power structure.

Sometimes the silo is more powerful than you. But almost any organizational silo can be pierced by an intrepid staffer looking to increase engagement.

Build these bridges based on creating results, getting things done, and routing around office politics that have things gummed up. You'll soon be known as the person who gets it done without trying to reinvent the organization first.

Launch Lessons from Five Guys Burgers and Fries

A new Five Guys burger restaurant just opened in our town, which I had been eagerly anticipating. I used to eat at the original restaurant in Arlington, VA, back in the early 1990s. When I stopped in at the Salisbury shop for the first time, they had been open for about four days.

I got my order and sat down at a table next to a guy who was wearing a Five Guys t-shirt but without the demeanor of someone who flips burgers. As I unwrapped my burger, I noticed it had all the wrong toppings on it. It must have shown on my face because suddenly I hear from the next table, "Not what you wanted?"

I said it wasn't; he confirmed my original order and then headed back to the kitchen. A few minutes later he was back with a new burger, another round of fries, and offered his apology.

Great customer service, no? I asked if he were the owner of the store and he said he was. He was doing something very smart for a business leader: He was sitting in his store during peak operations in the first week, watching how it went. Taking care of my individual burger was nice but the real important thing for him as the owner was that he had evidence of a broken process, poor training, or a simple one-off error. Such data he could act on, discovered during the shakedown cruise of his restaurant. The first cruise of a new ship is often called a shakedown because components that will fail early usually do so during that first cruise. The operators identify those problems, fix them, and then have confidence that the rest of the ship ought to hold up for the normal lifetime of those components.

The same principle applies to launching a new restaurant, a new product, or a new service. Pay a lot of attention during the shakedown run. Stay close to the action and see what isn't working as planned. Being close lets you catch these items quickly and do something about it.

Great Ideas Often Start Out Merely Good

When I was growing up in Columbus, Ohio, in the 1970s and 1980s, a new product line was introduced at the Big Bear grocery store: white label products. This was one of the first experiments with this new kind of consumer product.

The original white label products actually had white labels on them! A can of beans would have a white label and large text saying

"Beans." The idea was that the products were offered at a lower price point because they didn't have large marketing expenses built in to get people to buy them. (A huge part of the cost of many consumer food items is from marketing rather than raw materials and processing.)

Now white label products carry the brand of the supermarket selling them rather than just "Beans." It turns out that consumers like the comfort of a brand when making a buying decision, and adding the supermarket's brand to a product spreads out their marketing costs across more products, allowing either lower price points or higher profits (or a bit of both).

The overall lesson here is that providing true white label products was a good idea. It lowered prices significantly. But it wasn't a great idea until stores married it to their own brand.

Give your good ideas a shot and see how you can improve upon them. Most great ideas don't start out that way. Here are a few techniques you can use to see if a good product or service idea can be coaxed into a great one.

- **A good product in one market or segment might be great in another.** Try offering it to new people, perhaps tailoring it a bit for their unique needs and see what happens.

- **Add value to the product.** Microsoft's Word program started out as a mediocre word processor developed by another company. Microsoft bought it and continued to improve it until it dominated the market (owning the operating system certainly helped as well).

- **Market the product more effectively.** Perhaps your product is great; it's just that no one knows about it yet. Spread the word by focusing on value over features.

- **Combine with another product or service.** Combining two products can create greater value. People talked for years about the convergence of cell phones and computers until Apple finally nailed it with the iPhone.

- **Split it into multiple products or levels.** Some products might do better split into multiple offerings or by providing different investment levels. Freemium models are all the rage now, where a basic version of a web-based service is free and the more advanced benefits are only available to those who pay a fee.

If people are paying for an existing product or service, it means they are getting value. That is a great sign! It's a powerful base for you to build on to achieve a breakthrough success.

A Lone Wolf Is a Dead Wolf: Why You Need a Pack

Wolves are pack animals. A lone wolf quickly dies because without the support of a unified pack, he cannot bring down animals with which to feed himself.

Likewise, the lone wolf in an organization may have some limited success but it will be the exception rather than a consistent pattern.

You need your own wolf pack within and outside the organization. Whom do you rely on? Who can help you to get things done, to get that new product or campaign out the door? Extend this to external providers as well. The more useful people with whom you have relationships, the better you'll able to put together a team that cannot be beat.

And always remember that it should be a reciprocal relationship. No pack will have you long if you only take from others. Be generous with your assistance, advice, and aid when needed.

Organizational Politics Is a Means, Not an End

When I worked on staff at associations, I was quite good at navigating organizational politics, particularly later in my career. What I realized was that organizational politics is simply a means to an end rather than the point of the work. Once I figured that out, it was quite liberating and actually allowed me to engage in less politics while being more effective.

A critical part of managing organizational politics is understanding whether you are arguing about goals or about methods. Make this part of the conversation. Do we agree on what we are trying to achieve? If not, resolve that before moving on to determining how you will achieve it.

I have personally seen groups arguing about methodology when they had no agreement on what they were attempting to achieve. Going back to resolve the goal would often evaporate the original conflict because it was suddenly and obviously irrelevant to the clarified goal.

If you don't clarify the core of the argument like this, the only way to "win" is by retaining your turf. This rarely creates value for the organization or your mission.

Goals That Matter

My very first job when I moved to Washington, D.C. in the early 1990s was as a temp mailing sugar propaganda to schools across the country. The goal of the organization at the time was to promote the health benefits of natural sugar. While I found the idea of mailing sugar information to schools pretty amusing, especially the Spanish-language version titled "El Diente," it wasn't a goal I cared about at all. I actually felt somewhat guilty about it. Combined with the mind-numbing work, it was hard to stay motivated and I did precisely what was expected of me and no more. (I'm experiencing karmic payback now that I have two young children who love sugar!)

My next temp gig was filing paper event registration forms for an organization that helped companies relocate their employees more effectively. There was an international component to this, which I was very interested in since I had studied abroad in high school and college. The goal of relocation is to move people efficiently but also to do so in a way that enables the employee to become effective in the job as soon as possible. Much of this work actually focuses on supporting the family more than the employee.

This was something that I could get behind. I had personal experience with it and knew how valuable it was to people who were uprooting their lives to move across the world.

It was a goal that mattered to me. I worked hard, was offered a permanent position, and spent the next seven years moving through a half-dozen positions of increasing responsibility, constantly pushing to create new ways to achieve that goal.

What a difference a goal that mattered made to my career. I'm still exploring the path that those seven years opened up for me.

Engagement strategy works best when in pursuit of goals that matter. This is why goals that matter are critical if you want to be successful at creating powerful engagement at your organization. Engagement works only when it is in pursuit of goals that matter: goals that matter to you, your staff, your members, your customers, your donors, and anyone whose support you need to achieve them.

The Big List of Engagement Ideas and Their Values

B ELOW ARE IDEAS ON creating engagement in terms of time and money. They are grouped by value: micro, low, medium, and high. The value represented here is measured by that perceived by the individual engaging with the organization. Some items may have a relatively low value to the individual, yet still be of tremendous current value or future value to the organization when considered in the aggregate.

The point of this list is not to use all of these ideas at the same time but to provide grist for generating ideas on how to fill out and accelerate engagement with your constituents. If you choose to apply a different value to certain items than as they are presented below, that's fine and represents a strategic choice on your part. There is no single magic path; just choose the one to pursue that appears to have the best potential for success given your organization, goals, and environment.

Micro Levels of Value Engagement

Micro levels of value in terms of engagement are those bits of value that people can access passively without having to give data in exchange to the organization or other proactive effort. Few to none of these items will generate direct revenue and their best value is to serve as a conduit for new prospects to find the organization. Consider the following:

1. **Online display advertising**. Online ads can be posted on related websites, promoting low-value engagement opportunities (low value meaning the next step up from seeing an ad rather than a worthless impression). On some networks, the ads are relatively cheap compared to other channels, so consider investing when a site or network offers a focused and valuable audience.

2. **Post content to other related websites.** This can include sites such as blogs and industry publications, which have relevant audiences for your engagement curve. The content should feature an author or credit that mentions your organization, with a link to a dedicated landing page.

3. **Public service announcements**. These can run on local or national media. These count as micro value even though they can be quite expensive since the value they impart to any particular viewer is low and you are content for them to learn a bit about your priorities or to go to your website. Google is offering placement of video advertisements on television and cable at low prices that may provide some interesting opportunities to some organizations.

4. **Blogs, twitter, podcasts, video.** These represent the basic units of content in social media today. Content such as these are what typically get shared via social networking sites, email, and blogs. Make sure the content you post in these formats is designed to attract your best prospects for further engagement.

5. **Facebook fan page.** Setting up fan pages is relatively easy to do and provides an outpost for your organization in a very popular service. Do consider how you can support and monitor your fan page so that it is a sustainable activity and one that will provide good results for you.

6. **LinkedIn group.** Similar to the fan page on Facebook except in the much more straight-laced business environment of LinkedIn. These groups allow your members to have a badge on their profile from your organization and enable you to create a launch point for your organization on the site.

7. **Advertising on Google.** I'm sure you're familiar with Google's keyword-driven advertising by now. These can be very hit or miss but in some cases can be used to drive good prospects to you by posting ads on highly targeted search terms. Always test these campaigns closely to make sure they are driving the right traffic to you.

8. **Advertising on Facebook.** Just as with Google, you can place ads on Facebook that can be displayed to users based on very specific criteria that you can set in the campaign. Always consider where you will drive people who respond to the ad by clicking on it. What do you want them to do next?

9. **Mentions in media via public relations and other promotional efforts**. These reflect traditional public relations outcomes, where your organization is mentioned in the news media or other traditional outlet. Impact from exposure is often very hard to measure, but do consider what people are likely to come to you via each mention and how you can initially engage them via your website if they go to it later. The truth is that the vast majority of media mentions do not result in noticeable increases in web traffic.

10. **Advertising in traditional print media**. In this type of advertising, try to make a very specific offer and drive people to a web page or phone number where they can further engage with you. Consider the audience the publication reaches and the most relevant offer you can make to them via a print ad. Same goes for online ads on companion sites to the print publication.

11. **Direct mail promotions via rented lists.** This requires investment in both list rental and physical mailings but can drive good qualified candidates to you. The trick is in picking a highly relevant and high quality list for the offer you are going to make. Have a business plan for the promotion, including the offer you will make and your progression goals beyond it in order to calculate the value of the responses you'll receive.

Micro-Level to Low-Level Engagement Acceleration Tip

The best accelerant between micro- and low-level engagement is permission-based marketing. Gain permission from this new person to send further information of value to her. You can offer a free email newsletter (the first idea in the next section) or a free report. Whatever it is should be electronic so it can scale with no marginal cost and be of sufficient value so that a lot of people are willing to exchange their email address for it.

You can pursue Twitter followers and Facebook fans as well for acceleration, but old-fashioned email still trumps them both in terms of response for higher levels of engagement in many scenarios.

Low Levels of Value Engagement

Low levels of value engagement are the next step up from micro levels of value engagement, usually based upon the person taking a proactive step to further engage with your organization. Many of these options may be free in exchange for some time or information while others may have a relatively low price or fee associated with them. This is still a point at which your organization is prospecting for good candidates for higher levels of engagement.

1. **Free email newsletter subscription**. Another online classic, the free email newsletter. Target these at both your new prospects and your long-term participants. Always consider how you can provide great value via the newsletter to your target audiences while also providing specific next actions for them to take along the engagement curve with you.

2. **Free app.** This is a bit more cutting edge than the email newsletter. These small applications can run on a variety of smart phone operating systems now, with Apple's iPhone and Google's Android being the dominant players as of this writing. The best free apps provide value but also market higher-value opportunities with the publisher of the app, which might include a paid version with more content or features or other resources and benefits from the organization.

3. **Webinars.** These online events are very popular now with both paid and free offerings. These can be a great way to fill a gap in your engagement curve. Pricing is a key way to position it; low or no fee at the left and increasing the fee as you move to the right. People believe they get what they pay for, so don't be afraid to price a webinar offering at a high level if you can provide commensurate value!

4. **Job board or career center.** An online destination for posting of open positions from employers and resumés from job seekers. This can be a great next step for individuals who have recently come into your orbit.

5. **eBooks.** Electronic books or eBooks are a growing category, although they are still just a small chunk compared to traditional print publishing. However, they do provide great immediacy in serving needs and can be quite profitable since you do not have the overhead costs associated with large print runs. Consider creating shorter eBooks on narrow topics to fill niches in your curve.

6. **Publications.** This can include anything from books to periodicals to guides and reports. Just like with webinars, these items can be sold at the low end of the value continuum but you can also sell some items of high value at higher prices when warranted.

Low- to Medium-Engagement Acceleration Tip

Segmentation is the word of the day for acceleration from low- to medium-levels of engagement value. At this point, you should have enough data on people at the low level, based on their transactions with you and demographic data you have collected or inferred, that you can make highly specific and targeted appeals to them via mail, email, and phone. You can even use personalization on your website to provide targeted offers to them. Focus on what next steps, with you, at the medium level will provide the most value to those segments and put those messages in front of them on a regular basis, measuring results and adjusting as needed. Use data to drive acceleration at this transition point for best results.

Medium Levels of Value Engagement

Here is where we get to the prime levels of engagement, where people are making significant investments of time and money, from their perspective, in exchange for equal value from your organization.

1. **Membership.** This is a core offering and status for many organizations, even nonprofits other than associations. No need to go into great detail here but keep in mind that this is simply one stop along the engagement path with you,

albeit a very powerful one. Build great options before and after membership to maximize your impact and the value you deliver.

2. **Private social network.** This is the old-fashioned membership directory with a significant social media update. A private social network connects members with one another and allows them to collaborate just as they can on Facebook or LinkedIn except in a secure space under the brand of your organization. This can be quite valuable especially if your members are not comfortable making these kinds of connections via public networks and would see a lot of value in a private space just for their field or industry.

3. **Subscription to online content.** This is an offering of online content in a monthly subscription model. For a certain amount of dollars per month, subscribers get access to new content as it is added (which could include podcasts, webinars, video, documents, and other resources) as well as the full archive of past offerings. This can be a wonderful complement to membership or stepping-stone before membership. It can also serve as a valuable offering to those who do not qualify to be a member of the organization, yet still want to receive value.

4. **Meetings and events.** Another classic offering from associations and other types of nonprofits focused on dissemination of knowledge, training, development, and other activities. The key consideration in engagement with events such as this is to map out which earlier activities indicate they are a great candidate for your events and to look at post event

opportunities for further engagement. Don't let your event be a single engagement event, make it part of a process.

5. **Grassroots advocacy actions.** Some might consider grassroots advocacy efforts as a lower-value opportunity but in my experience, people who are more firmly engaged with the organization are likely to act on your behalf with the state and federal government bodies and other advocacy targets. Evaluate your most active supporters, see what they have in common, and then recruit more of the same. Also consider what they should do next with you. Don't be afraid to make this an integral process of all the value you have to offer, rather than just a silo in the organization.

6. **Speaking and writing opportunities.** Speaking at your events and writing in your publications often goes hand-in-hand with membership or other constituents with whom the organization engages. As I suggest above, expand your thinking about these activities to accelerate engagement to and through them.

7. **Special supporter status.** Charities that do a lot of fundraising often use special supporter statuses effectively to recognize and incent higher levels of giving. Consider how you might use them in your organization to recognize those who have made significant contributions of some form. This recognition is validating for the individual in question but also creates exemplars for others to model in their own interactions with you.

8. **Serve on a committee, task force, or other volunteer activity.** These mid-level volunteer opportunities often cement

a member's or supporter's relationship with the organization
for their professional or charitable life. Time is truly the most
valuable asset they can give, since we all have a finite amount
of time on the planet. In building your engagement curve,
consider where you can create volunteer opportunities to
help build engagement and long-term relationships while
also serving your mission and providing a highly satisfying
experience to the person working with you.

Medium- to High-Engagement Acceleration Tip

Moving people from medium to high levels of engagement is
all about the relationship they have with your organization and key
people within it. Enlist both staff and leadership to help graduate your
best candidates to higher levels. You can identify them by using a set
of profiles that help you understand what they look like at lower levels
of engagement and then focus your efforts on those best candidates.
Talk to them, understand their priorities and goals, and help them
decide which of your next set of engagement options makes the most
sense for them.

High Levels of Value Engagement

The pinnacle of engagement. These opportunities may seem
rather traditional and old school, but they are still very high-value
activities and roles that most organizations make a part of how they
pursue their missions.

1. **Serve as a senior leader of the organization.** These activities
   can include serving as the chair of a committee or task force up

to serving on the board of directors. In most nonprofit organizations these are critical leadership positions that require relationships to be built over time and nurtured to get the best people on board.

2. **Exhibit at tradeshow**. For groups that put on meetings and events, tradeshow exhibitors are often what make the whole endeavor profitable or even possible to hold. They spend significant money to engage with your attendees while underwriting a lot of the expense of the educational offerings. I consider this to be a high level of engagement.

3. **Rainmaker**. Charities and service organizations often have a small cadre of people who help bring in major donors and sponsors. Even associations can have people in this critical role. While they may give significant gifts themselves, they generate far more by the people they attract to the organization on your behalf.

4. **Large sponsorships or gifts**. This is the rain! People who are strong financial supporters of the organization are participating at a high level of engagement with you. Even corporate sponsorships have an individual who signs off on them. It's always about strong relationships at this level.

5. **Award fellowship, emeritus status, or other recognition of significant achievement.** Finally, recognition of lifetime contributions and achievements is often one of the top honors any organization can bestow. The actual time or money involved in this is low but the recognition reflects the total effort they have made in the past.

The above list is certainly not comprehensive, as there are literally limitless possibilities for your engagement path. Many of these are not radically new ideas, either. What is new, though, is considering the complete picture of how you build engagement with your constituents and growing it with strategic intent. This list should help you to fill out your curve and give you a jumping-off point for innovating your own unique offerings that best serve your needs and goals.

INDEX

About the Author

C. David Gammel, CAE, now executive director of the Entomological Society of America and formerly a long time consultant and speaker, has been quoted in *The New York Times, The Washington Post,* and *Wired* magazine on issues such as social media, web strategy, and the impact of the web on business. He is the author of the book, *Online and On Mission: Practical Web Strategy for Breakthrough Results,* as well as the one you are holding right now!

David has spoken internationally to Fortune 500, small business, and nonprofit executives on diverse subjects from web strategy and technology to international business assignments and online culture.

Throughout his career, David has helped organizations maximize engagement by increasing the time and money members invest in their products, services, and mission. His consulting clients included everything from a start-up purchased by Google to mature technology companies to some of the world's leading nonprofit organizations. He has worked as an executive at leading healthcare, scientific, and business associations. You can reach David at david@highcontext.com or via his website at www.highcontext.com.